Rescue Machines At Work

Rescue Helicopters

By Hal Rogers

The Child's World® Inc. ◆ Eden Prairie, Minnesota

Published by The Child's World®, Inc.
7081 W. 192 Ave.
Eden Prairie, MN 55346

Design and Production:
The Creative Spark, San Juan Capistrano, CA

Photos: © 1998 David M. Budd Photography

Library of Congress Cataloging-in-Publication Data

Rogers, Hal, 1966-
     Rescue helicopters / by Hal Rogers.
        p. cm.
     Summary: A brief introduction to rescue helicopters, what they do,
and how they work.
     ISBN 1-56766-657-4 (lib. bdg. : alk. paper)
     1. Helicopters in search and rescue operations—Juvenile
literature. 2. Helicopters—Juvenile literature. [1. Helicopters.]
2. Rescue work.] I. Title.
TL553.8.R64   1999
629.133'352—dc21
                                         99-20856
                                           CIP
                                               AC

Contents

On the Job

On the job, a rescue helicopter takes sick people to the hospital. It can travel very quickly. It is like a flying **ambulance.**

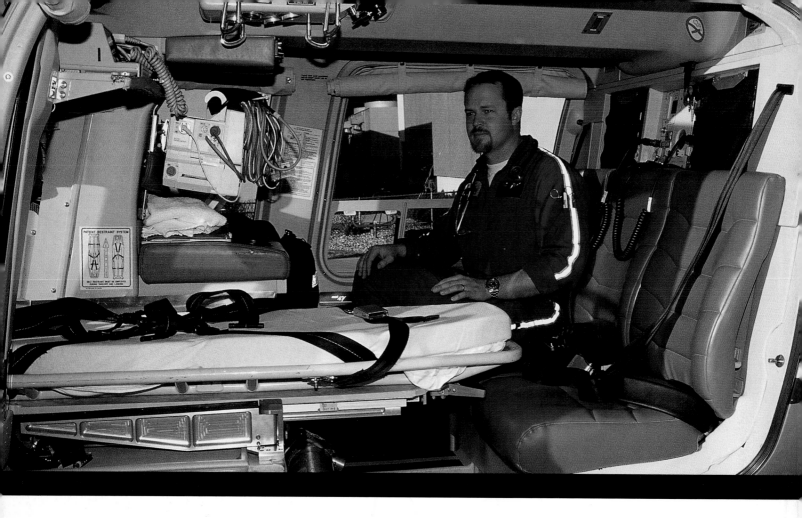

There is a special bed in the helicopter's

cabin. It is for the **patient.** A nurse sits

next to the patient during the flight.

The pilot sits in the **cockpit.**

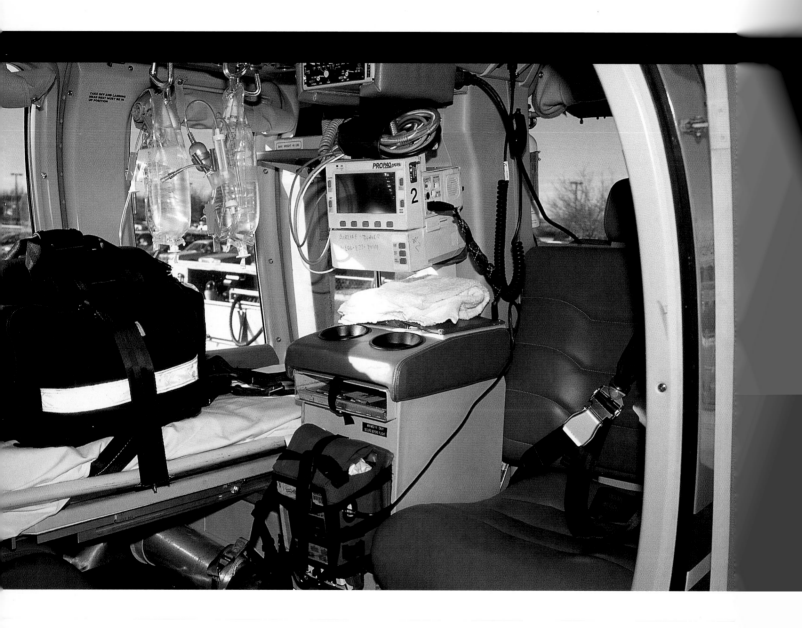

A rescue helicopter has many special machines. The nurse uses the machines to take care of the patient.

There are **rotors** on top of the helicopter.

They spin around and around. The rotors

move very fast to make the helicopter fly.

There is another rotor on the helicopter's
tail. It helps the helicopter fly straight.

Stabilizers on the tail make the ride smooth.

A rescue helicopter has two bright lights on the bottom. They help the pilot see at night.

The pilot fills the helicopter's tank with fuel. It can fly for almost three hours. Then it must stop for more fuel.

Climb Aboard!

Would you like to see where the pilot sits?

The cockpit has many **instruments.**

It also has a **radio.** The pilot uses the radio

to talk to people on the ground. **Controls**

help the pilot steer. They also help him take

off and land.

Up Close

The inside

1. The instruments

2. The controls

3. The radio

The outside

1. The rotors

2. The stabilizers

3. The cockpit

4. The cabin

Glossary

ambulance (AM-byoo-lentz)
An ambulance is a truck used to carry sick or injured people. A rescue helicopter is like a flying ambulance.

cabin (KAB-en)
A cabin is the space inside a helicopter where passengers sit. The nurse and the patient ride in the rescue helicopter's cabin.

cockpit (KAWK-pit)
The cockpit is the place where a helicopter's pilot sits. The pilot flies the helicopter from the cockpit.

controls (kun-TROLZ)
Controls are tools used to help make something work. A helicopter pilot uses the controls to take off, to steer, and to land.

instruments (IN-stre-mintz)
Instruments are tools used to help fly a helicopter. Instruments show the pilot how high the helicopter is flying, how fast it is going, and many other important things.

patient (PAY-shunt)
A patient is someone who needs medical care. Doctors and paramedics take care of patients.

radio (RAYD-ee-o)
A radio is a special machine on a helicopter. The pilot uses the radio to talk to people on the ground.

rotors (ROHT-erz)
Rotors are long metal parts on a helicopter. Rotors spin around very quickly to make a helicopter fly.

stabilizers (STAY-buh-lye-zerz)
Stabilizers are metal parts on the tail of a helicopter. They make the helicopter fly more smoothly.